nothi
bu
m

ng

t the

usic

Documentaries from nightclubs, dance halls & a tailor's shop in Dakar

1974—1992

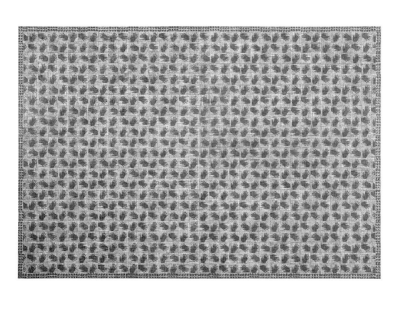

Thulani Davis

to the artists
& dharma guides
who coax us
minute by minute
from retold pasts
& possible futures
ever
to the present
moment

Grateful acknowledgments for poems reprinted from: Davis, *All the Renegade Ghosts Rise*, Anemone Press, Washington, DC, 1978: "Cicatrix," "He Didn't Give Up/ He Was Taken," "On Five Compositions of Roscoe Mitchell," "Rogue & Jar," "Storyville," "Zoom (the Commodores)"; Parallels - Danspace Project Platform 2012: "For Ishmael Houston-Jones"; Davis, *Playing the Changes*, Wesleyan University Press, Middleton, CT, 1978: "As I Fly Over This Time," "Bad Brains, a Band," "C.T.'s Variation," "Mecca Flats 1907"; *Village Voice*: "Backstage Drama," "T- Monious"; *X-75-Vol. I*, Henry Threadgill, "Side A" & "Side B."

Poems from this work that have been set to music: "He didn't give up/He was taken": for voice and chamber ensemble, Henry Threadgill, on *Pilgrimage*, Roscoe Mitchell, New Chamber Ensemble, CD, Lovely Music, 1993; "C.T.'s Variation," set as "Some Springs," for voice and chamber ensemble, by Anthony Davis, 1987; "A Man's Tailor" and "Leaving Goree": composition for chamber ensemble, voices and dancers, Bernadette Speach, "Baobab 4," MusicVistas and P.S. 122, New York, NY, 1994; "Mecca Flats," "Back Stage Drama," "Bad Brains," and other works, performed by Thulani Davis, music by Anthony Davis, *Thulani*, a film by Doris Chase, 1984.

Published by Blank Forms Editions in Brooklyn, NY

Cover photograph:
   Anthony Barboza,
   Folk City, New York, NY, 1980

Preliminary page image:
   McArthur Binion
   Hand:Work
   2018
   oil paint stick and paper on board
   96" x 144" x 2"

Design by Alec Mapes-Frances
Printed by Ofset Yapımevi, Istanbul

ISBN 978-1-7337235-6-5

Blank Forms
468 Grand Avenue #3D
Brooklyn, NY 11238

Editor-in-Chief: Lawrence Kumpf
Deputy Editor: Joe Bucciero

Blank Forms is supported by the Robert Rauschenberg Foundation and the Andy Warhol Foundation for the Visual Arts

blankforms.org

CONTENTS

ACKNOWLEDGMENTS

I have heard this music in a lot of clubs that no longer exist, opera houses in Italy that will stand another hundred years, parks in Manhattan, Brooklyn, L.A., San Francisco, and Washington, DC as well as on Goree Island and in Harare, Zimbabwe. Some of it was in lofts in lower Manhattan now inhabited by millionaires, crowded bistros in Paris that are closed, and legendary sites like Mandel Hall and the Apollo, radio studios, recording studios, and my many homes.

Many of the poems here were performed with a number of musicians in different improvising configurations including Pheeroan akLaff, Dwight Andrews, Kelvyn Bell, Arthur Blythe, Ronnie Burrage, Marilyn Crispell, Anthony Davis, Marty Ehrlich, Henry Grimes, Fred Hopkins, Joseph Jarman, Oliver Lake, Myra Melford, David Murray, James Newton, Jeffrey Schanzer, Bernadette Speach, Cecil Taylor, and Phillip Wilson. As it has turned out, over the years some of these same poems were set to music and performed by others.

This book emerged as a joyous consolation for a grief that was new in the winter of 2019. I sent in the manuscript this year, 2020, a month before the COVID-19 pandemic became the all-consuming, grievous, and maddening experience it has been. Soon corporate advertisers were peppering our screens with soft

messages of caring in this "unique time," referring to
something we are unlikely to forget. So it took shape
while everyone working on it altered all the ways in
which we go through ordinary life. My classes shifted
to my dining room table; seniors and graduates finished
school only on paper. Being an older person, I began
getting notices of people who did not survive this virus.
Live music became videos of Brian Stokes Mitchell
belting "The Impossible Dream" out of his window at the
7 p.m. hour when New Yorkers cheer first responders and
medical workers. Or music stars at home playing into
laptops. Some of those who worked on this book were not
even born when I was sitting in clubs or lofts writing in
notebooks or on napkins. And then the murder of George
Floyd: the American Spring began and they worked
during the day and were joyously in the streets at night
and I want to thank them for persisting despite arrest
or as police turned up in the narrow brownstone streets
of their neighborhoods. Live music became crowds of
masked protestors massed in the streets singing "Lean
on Me." Or songs heard live here in Wisconsin by
students who only knew them from footage of students in
the South more than 50 years ago.

The poet Steve Timm, who works upstairs from me at
the University of Wisconsin–Madison but whom I met in
New York at a celebration of Cecil Taylor at the Whitney
Museum, retyped this manuscript when I could not.
Lawrence Kumpf and Adrian Rew and those at Blank
Forms whom I do not know kept it moving with close
attention to detail, graciousness with my ideas, and an
enthusiasm that is still inspiring. I was delighted to meet
the gifted Tobi Haslett and am proud to have him think
about my poems. My dear friend Jessica Hagedorn and
I have had many laughs recalling our willfully blithe

adventures on two coasts "back when," and what we were wearing at the time. The laughter was a balm. So it is with more than an ordinary gratitude I thank her for taking the time to write about this work. Faith Childs's astute advice and friendship continue to sustain me. McArthur Binion and his assistant Elizabeth Smarz were generous and patient with my inquiries to look at images of McArthur's work. The titles of his recent painting series apply to this kind of work as well, especially *Handwork*. My poems come from pens and hands that luckily keep recovering from every disability computer keyboards dish out. And thanks to Alesia Alexander, my research assistant whose archive cataloguing allowed me to put those hands on these poems.

One day a little voice will tell you:

Put down the knitting
The book and the broom.
It's time for a holiday.
Life is a Cabaret, old chum,
Come to the Cabaret.[1]

I wish you all the live music you can get your hands on.

Thulani Davis
June 25, 2020
Madison, Wisconsin

---

1   *Cabaret*, Kander and Ebb, 1966.

FOREWORD:
GIVE ME THE ROMANCE AND THE ZOOM
Jessica Hagedorn

Thulani has been my poet sister artist comrade for nearly fifty years. We met in San Francisco one night in either 1971 or 1972—young poets with flash and sass, opinionated and full of ourselves. We were reading at the Western Addition Cultural Center with several other poets, fiery types like Roberto Vargas, Serafin Syquia, Miz Redbone, maybe even Avotcja and Marvin X. Buriel Clay, a local writer and community activist, had organized the program and brought us all together. I was new at doing readings and didn't know anyone there. I remember being nervous and excited. There wasn't much of an audience, but being a part of this dynamic group felt like a very big deal.

Dim lights. A podium, a mic, rickety folding chairs. Thulani was one of the last to read. The quiet, incantatory power of her voice and the bravado of her poem got me.

I am Brown
I am a child of the third world
my hair black n long
my soul slavetraded n nappy
yellow brown-Safronia
in this world, illegitimate seed...

On her way out the door that night, Thulani made a cryptic comment about the tattered, patched-up jeans I had on. Whatever she said made me laugh. We became friends—hung out at her place on Oak Street, smoked Kools and Gitanes, and *talked.* Talk, talk, and more talk. We were curious and passionate about everything, from Jimi Hendrix to Anna May Wong to Jean-Luc Godard and Tennessee Williams. Thulani turned me on to The Original Last Poets, Bill Gunn's *Ganja and Hess*, Archie Shepp & Jeanne Lee's "Blasé," Ishmael Reed's *Mumbo Jumbo*, Pedro Pietri's *Puerto Rican Obituary*, Nikki Giovanni's "Ego Tripping," and Amiri Baraka's "Beautiful Black Women."

We found ourselves suddenly being invited to participate in marathon benefit readings for righteous causes. Free Angela Davis, Stop the War in Vietnam, Support the Farmworkers, Save the I-Hotel. The audiences were huge and could be disruptive at these politically charged events. Our token status wasn't lost on us. Ken Kesey, Allen Ginsberg, and Lawrence Ferlinghetti were the stars the people were there to see and hear. No matter. We showed up with our poems and our swagger, determined to have fun. Maybe, just maybe, we'd win the crowd over.

My world kept expanding. Thulani introduced me to her East Coast running buddies, who came out for a visit and ended up staying awhile. Brainy, arty, fabulous people like Arnim, Monsieur Henri, Mother Popcorn, and the poet Ntozake Shange. Ntozake and Thulani met as students at Barnard and became great friends. She would become a significant figure in our writing lives.

It was a freaky-deaky time, in a freaky-deaky city filled with duende and strife. Chaos and creativity reigned. You could burn out quickly, die anytime. We were immersed in language and music. Writing felt potent, dangerous, and necessary. As we grew bolder and more ambitious, collaborations with musicians, visual artists, and dancers began happening with more frequency. Thulani left the Bay Area in 1973. New York City beckoned, in all its grimy splendor.

Fast forward to 1977. Thulani, Ntozake, and I create *Where the Mississippi Meets the Amazon,* a poetry and music cabaret show that was produced and presented by Joseph Papp at the Public Theater that same year. The title derives from a poem by Ntozake, and the ever-evolving script was made up of poems written by each of us. We called ourselves The Satin Sisters and performed with an all-star band of kick-ass musicians: David Murray on saxophone, Anthony Davis on piano, Fred Hopkins on bass, Pheeroan akLaff on drums, and Michael Gregory Jackson on guitar and vocals. The Public's Martinson Theater was transformed into a gritty nightclub, with charming waitstaff serving drinks. (A forerunner to Joe's Pub, perhaps.) And there we were—glammed-up and talk-singing mystifying poems while channeling Chaka Khan. Somehow, it all worked. *Where the Mississippi Meets the Amazon* ran for four astonishing months. Nothing like it had ever been done before, and nothing like it ever since.

A couple of months before the COVID-19 pandemic shut New York City down, I re-read the script for *Mississippi/Amazon* and listened to an archival recording of one of our final performances. I'm glad I did. One of the high points of my listening session came towards the end, with Thulani's rendition of "Zoom (The Commodores)." It's my all-time favorite poem of hers. Written before video-conferencing became the new normal, Thulani's "Zoom" is a lusty poem you can dance to—a celebration of humanity and "the love that can keep death waiting." Her best line never fails to crack me up: "Talking trash is one of the lost arts." Funny, poignant, oh so true.

A lot of people know Thulani as a masterful writer in multiple genres. They've read her fiction and non-fiction, they've seen the movies she's written, they've attended her operas and plays. *Nothing but the Music* brings our attention to Thulani's grounding as a poet, allowing us to appreciate her body of work in a fresh and startling way. With this new book, "Zoom (The Commodores)" has claimed its rightful place alongside brilliant poems about Cecil Taylor, Henry Threadgill, Thelonious Monk, and the Art Ensemble of Chicago.

How cool is that?

May 21, 2020
New York City

Darting through these poems is an answer to a
question, posed by multiple and overlapping waves of
Black artists: How do you account for the dynamism at
the heart of Black expression, and its centrality to the
wider culture it's been forced to resist? To phrase the
question this way invokes the figure of the fighter: not
the pedant or the philistine, but the militant, advancing
swiftly across a field of possibilities. As a writer, Thulani
Davis has adopted an array of canny tactics. Journalist,
librettist, novelist, historian, performer, memoirist,
poet: these are her many roles, gathered over a lifetime
of collaboration and productive flux. In this book the
identities are braided into a single ethos; *Nothing but the
Music* marries poetry and struggle, and presents their
reciprocity as essential to style:

> *"That's just like Angola," Terri chimed,*
> *"Sometimes it's not who but what, sometimes not what*
>   *but who."*
> *I'm trying to talk to these people about this race riot—*
> *someone is walking on the bar*
> *and everyone of us belongs even now to Miami,*
> *to people we have never seen.*

Note the stray strand of dialogue, the wobble of "who" and "what," the powerful unseen "people," and the "riot" slashing through. This is a mind which bears the imprint of revolutions in art and politics, someone for whom the "avant-garde" is fiercely bolted to both its meanings. Born in Hampton, Virginia, in 1949, Davis passed through the successive crucibles of the Civil Rights movement, Black Power, the New Left, feminism, and the striking bohemian ferment of San Francisco and New York from the '70s on, all of which have left their marks on her multifarious practice. But the above lines, from "Back Stage Drama (for Miami)," take place in the time before or after the spectacle onstage; rather than capture a performance, the poem unfurls within a glamorous seclusion. "They all like to hang out," read the first two lines. "Thinking is rather grim to them." But thinking hacks its way in—advances and invades—inflecting the whole scene and establishing its limits. Angola, riots, people we've never seen: There's a vivid, thrashing world beyond the comforts of this drama, the world that "backstage" retreats from and seeks to guard against, but for which it must finally prepare.

These are backstage poems. By which I mean that they issue from a place of sophisticated doubleness, slung between intimate complication and the blast of political life. The realms clash and melt in music, and especially in Black music—which is not the subject of this book so much as its ultimate horizon. Jazz, punk, R&B: Black performance here figures as an intricate, varied practice as well as a thrumming psychic rhythm, something that both collapses and expands the subjectivity that consumes it. "Working in new / forms, stepping / outside tradition is / like taking a solo," opens "For Ishmael Houston-Jones." Most of these pieces were directly inspired by shows—by Henry Threadgill, Cecil Taylor, Art

Ensemble of Chicago, or a horn-player on the street—and are followed by a date and place. This little annotation slits the poem open; the world comes trickling in. It's a reminder, too, that this particular poet for many years composed write-ups and conducted interviews while on staff at the *Village Voice*, such that the Black music was not just a private pleasure but planted at the front of her life, its breaking news. *1980, 122nd Street, New York; December 16, 1987*—the latitude and longitude of a critical sensibility.

That sensibility is pitched against a backdrop of thrilling, roaring history, full of bold questions, difficult answers, ambivalent heroes, and eclipsed hopes. In the 1960s, Larry Neal's dream for the Black Arts Movement was to produce an un-alienated expression, one aligned—reunited—with what was happening in the street. The Black feminism that followed deepened and broadened that understanding, as it grasped at what June Jordan called the "the intimate face of universal struggle." Davis's work as a poet is driven by both of these impulses: that art should be fastened to politics, and politics to the texture of life. The result is a marvelous and subtle warping of our sense of social scale. "this is not about romance & dream / it's about a terrible command performance of the facts," she writes in her tribute to Cecil Taylor. These poems dilate and contract, working to convey affection and wryness, about the People in the abstract and the people on the block:

> *I know there's only minutes left*
> *have to tune in*
> *find out if it's a riot in LA*
> *or if we can still dance*
> *to Teddy Pendergrass*

& songs we hummed before
they made love stories
called "Damage"
Al Green is crying,
Aw baby, did you mean that?

was the jury hung in LA?
did they acquit somebody in LA?
will we burn it down on Saturday
or dance to the Rhythm Revue
the not too distant past
when we thought we'd live on?

The tone slides into, and out of, an elaborately mediated anguish, all the more poignant for its manifestation as an invisible set of sounds: Al Green, Teddy Pendergrass, and the nattering dominance of the radio, which lets you simply "tune in" to "find out if it's a riot in LA." The end of "It's Time for the Rhythm Revue" is marked by the words, "1992, Brooklyn, NY"—the year, but not the city, of the acquittal of the policemen who beat Rodney King. The event crash-landed into public consciousness but is refracted in this poem through the prisms of humor and denial. The L.A. riots do not figure here as some flabbergasting rupture. They are expressions of a people moving, in harmony and under fire: They take their place on a wrenching continuum, which includes Black song and dance.

Nothing but the Music, then, is a coy title. It pretends to bracket the whole world only to assert the capaciousness of what Davis's late husband, the jazz musician Joseph Jarman, referred to as Great Black Music. There is nothing but the music because that music is fiercely and irrefutably expansive, a quality painfully thrust upon it by the experience of history. Everything is the music: struggle, bafflement, war, love. The pain these things precipitate is the music, too. Hence the voluptuous shift in register that is a hallmark of these poems. "Bad Brains, a Band" takes the legendary DC punks as a prompt to trace the outlines of gender and class. The piece swings from "the idea they think must scare people to death" to the melancholy observation that "he wanted to buy me a Bentley / because he didn't want to be black." And it is something like this melancholy—not as a private indulgence but as an aesthetic inheritance—that animates "Mecca Flats 1907." This poem in many ways exemplifies the themes that flow through this collection. The Mecca Flats was a famous apartment complex on the South Side of Chicago. Originally built as lodgings for wealthy visitors to the 1892 World's Columbian Exposition, it was converted into apartments before being razed in 1952, over the protestations of the black people who lived there. "Mecca Flat Blues," the song by James Louis Blythe, had established the building's place within the symbolism of Black art, its salacious verses making news in its day; Gwendolyn Brooks's *In the Mecca* (1968) would fortify that place. *In the Mecca* marked Brooks's entrée into the Black Arts Movement; the building itself served as, among other things, a microcosm for the complications of the Black Power to which she had just dedicated her work. These legacies surge through Davis's poem, too, which is stalked and amplified by lost voices, macabre images, muffled histories, and piano notes. The poem marks a physical location and the Black music that enlivens it, drawing into its forcefield a host of spiritual resources. These propel this particular writer, and tell the story of her people, who have always lived on "the south side of anywhere / That's blue."

June 2020

nothing but the music

FOR ISHMAEL HOUSTON-JONES

Working in new
forms, stepping
outside tradition is
like taking a solo ...

The artist breathes
in a heap of air, the
chords, tones, and
even the structure of
his or her world and ...

And then in one
concentrated
moment moves
and breathes
out ...

The sound becomes
a shape, a dance, a
configuration of what
we know that we have
not seen or heard that
way ...

but still with
that sensibility that
taught the world how
to solo—solitary
yet communal,
disciplined and free.

1982, 122nd Street, New York.

On this landscape
Like a thin air
Hard to breathe
Behind God's back
I see the doors
But few can enter
Soot flakes crowd the view
Down narrow jagged streets
Women's eyes peer
Out windows, porches
Watching for passers-by
Piano playing it: C A D# E
I went up there
Went to the south side
Of a town wide open
That grips you like a vice
On this landscape like thin air
I see the doors
I want to enter
Honkytonk and barrelhouse
Sweet relief
Behind God's back
Where few are so many
And the talk is loud
Where love might be this old friend
Sportin' in the door
Take me to the south side
Of anywhere that's blue
Put me near the ones and nines
The five'll get you two
I like the way the hips curve
And the shirt looks new

He could bring it over here
Piano playing it: C A D# E
Inside this landscape
The back of Mecca Flats
The south side of anywhere
That's blue

1978, Brooklyn, NY.

this is not about romance & dream
it's about a terrible command performance of the facts
of time & space & air
it breathes of journey/brilliant light journey
up thru the where was & who lived
it works those melodies to their pith/to their pulp
it fists & palms the last dirt roads
of lives that have to give out before they give up
bury me with music and don't say a word
the only preacher is a poet
the text I have not read
but heard screamin' out of saxophones
I have heard this music
ever since I can remember/I have heard this music
facing the dinge of spots & twofers
in the night/music/in the night/music have I lived

ripple stamp & beat/ripple peddlin'
stomps taps of feet slick poundin' out
tonal distinctions between/keys & sticks
between funk & the last love song/he romps in beauty
the player plays/Mr. Taylor plays
delicate separate licks of poems
brushes in tones lighter & tighter/closer in space
sweet sassy melodies lean in
givin' in at the knees/where it's at
to get that stuff/sweet sassy melodies
hittin' fast off the top of the stride
sweet sassy melodies knowin' what it takes
to even walk those bottom notes/stomps
on those bottoms yes he's been there he knows
the man struggles/bends the meanness

takes hold of the meanness of a ditch beatin
sweet sassy/man you gotta wrestle that joy
dig your heels rapid on hard ground/over & over
straighten your back and grab hold of the blindness
of stars 'fore you let go
this is not about romance
this is the real stuff
commandin' a state/of the meanness/of the sweetness
of the time it takes/of the space it needs
of the weight of old air/it breathes
& sees like knives thru the thickness of flesh
& the blindness of our very selves
I have heard this music
ever since I can remember/I have heard this music

April 15, 1975, Five Spot, New York. The Cecil Taylor Unit: Cecil Taylor,
Jimmy Lyons, Andrew Cyrille.

they always play it different in new york/fast city
nothin clean about the place
no such thing as one hand clapping
or like the purity of only one horn & the hall
you can hear it talking
like hard times & bent slugs
fast city in ya music
hear it cry fast moanful cries
violins step in/I hear ya fast city
music of the way back/way out ahead
of the knife-fendered traffic
of the lowceiling five flights blues
in peeling browns & rust-edged dangers
I hear ya fast city
bursting all through the pure
with the lost gone gangster tones
blast me back through the scag & jump of it
the rob & steal of it
to the stomp joy and sweet completion of it
in remembrance of the brightness
the song of one sound slapping snapping & grabbing
the round of it/the last lost found/the hollow of it
nonaah/long knowing/I say it says
I hear ya fast city
long gone bipblap kick rumble
kicks and rumbles back again
loose hairs of discontent
fall like lint upon the players coats
one eats oranges & shoots seeds down the slide
one leans big boy falls against his chest
he lets his feet fly and march
one says he has true dreads

plays stripper funk in the spaces
sweet intensity/I hear ya/fast city
pluggin on the deaf insistence of blind horsemen
stompin' Dumas' clouds
out from under/in sky/stomping
the music/splattered with spit & sweat
the gone ones' blood

February 8, 1976, Studio Rivbea, New York. The players: Roscoe Mitchell,
Julius Hemphill, Phillip Wilson, Joseph Bowie, Richard Muhal Abrams,
Leroy Jenkins, George Lewis.

A   1. Tahquemenon
        2. Tecumseh
        3. Olobo
        4. Eckter five

B   5. Nonaah (ensemble)

BACK STAGE DRAMA (FOR MIAMI)

They all like to hang out.
Thinking is rather grim to them.
Snake & Minnie
who love each other dearly
drink in different bars,
ride home in separate cars.
They like to kiss goodnight
with unexplored lips.
They go out of town
to see each other open.
This they do for no one else.
Minnie does it all for God.
Snake does it all for fame.
Back stage is where they play their games.
(That's why I know their business.)
I was gonna talk about a race riot.
They said they'd never played that town.
Fleece told me he'd seen an old movie—
a black town attacking a white one.
Sidney Poitier was the young doctor
accused, abused and enraged.
There were Ossie Davis & Woody Strode,
Ruby Dee & a hundred unknowns,
also Sapphire's mama as a maid.
"What was Sapphire's mama's name?" said Inez.
I was going to talk about a race riot
but we were stuck on Kingfish's mother-in-law.
Minnie kissed Snake so he'd forget about that.
I said, "they're mad, they're on the bottom going down/
stung by white justice in a white town
and then there's other colored people
who don't necessarily think they're colored people

taking up the middle/leaving them the ground."
"That's just like the dreads, the Coptics and the
      Manleyites,"
one of the drunks said too loud,
"I and I know," say he.
Snake yelled, "Are you crazy? No, it ain't and no we don't!"
"That's just like Angola," Terri chimed,
"Sometimes it's not who but what, sometimes not what
      but who."
I'm trying to talk to these people about this race riot—
someone is walking on the bar
and everyone of us belongs even now to Miami,
to people we have never seen.
Pookie & Omar want to know what's going on.
They always do
'cause they're always in the bathroom
when it's going on.
They do everything together and not for God
and not for fame but for love.
At least that's what their records say.
They are a singing group that's had 13 Pookies.
Omar asked me, "What do you want to say?"
Inez interrupts, "She don't know what to say,
      she just wants to say something.
I understand that."
The 13th Pookie chirped, "This race riot sounds like all
the other race riots."
Fleece said, "And you sound like 12 other Pookies, Pookie."
I am still trying to talk about this race riot.
Minnie looked up and said, "We don't have anywhere
to put any more dead."
Snake put on his coat to leave, "We never did,
      we never did."

1980, 122nd Street, New York.

27

X-75-VOL. I, HENRY THREADGILL "SIDE A (SIR SIMPLETON/CELEBRATION)"

at the turning of the day
in these winters/in the city's bottomless streets
it seems sometimes we live behind god's back
we/the life blood
of forgotten places/unhallowed ground
sometimes in these valleys
turning the corner of canyons
now filled with blinding light streams
caught between this rock & a known hard place
sometimes in an utter solitude
a chorale/a sweetness/makes us whole & never lost
a high string calls back
that sorrow song that had no words
a song the old folks knew sighs like a violin
the lowest bass notes all agree
there is no sadness/there is only a pause
without introduction or explanation
a plucking/a motion/this music
clips the heartbeat & eases
eases like the smoothest dude on the block
into the street/into where we live
gathers the moments into joyousness
even as Mingus leaves us
grappling the thick rhythms
of how we insist on life
even as he leaves us in those moans
those minor chords of elegance & desire
quartets of basses push our hips & lift our feet
& keep it rollin' & keep it rollin'
cat gut on octos & piccolos
& old fat stand-up walk thrus

bend your back & lay into it basses
basses/keep it rollin'
running over rhythms like the old steel strings
like John Heard's four pairs of hands
old delta nods & glances pick up our feet
give these streets a little bend & play
here we are smiling
the fluted alto of woman earth
pushes weariness aside
birds occur where there were none
haunting calls court us
conjure & spell like love come back
giving a spring to the dance
of who we are/unexpected beauty
beauty we have known ourselves to be
like reaching old age & infancy in a breath
of this is the music
knowing we can't be us
& be afraid of who we are

January 1979, Brooklyn, NY.

X-75-VOL. I, HENRY THREADGILL
"SIDE B (AIR SONG/FE FI FO FUM)"

a reach/a flight
first cry/first praise
how we have loved flight
sung Solomon's song
how we have known
the sweetness of this choir
is making the air one's own
a reach/a flight
an ascension/the spirit knows
here in the hour of the tiger
before the sun eclipses last
in this era/are flutes in chorus
and voice in flight forever
singular language of the sun-lit faces
mistress of the blinded sages
music keeps us up on where we are
with a spine of bass keys/backbonin'
the bottom/the ole southside is there
or saloons in California
& then, of course, "the jazz life" joints
we smile after hours on the lower east side
steppin' & stompin' & steppin' & stridin'
where dairy bars hop with hip tales
all the living legends gather
over record dates/historic gigs/dope stories
music intrigue & sudden disappearances
"rough life"/"no breaks" unrecorded
among boppin' feet/gippin' hips
reviving the Shepp look/itself reviving
the Prez/Bird style/we live on the hard past
every address once inhabited

by Morgan or Dolphy/Jones or Joans
or just four amazing flights up/
from Phebe's/Brownie's/avenues A B C D
yeah where Slugs has been known to be
Polish egg stores & all the soggy sawdust
claim history like record joints claim
"bootleg Hendrix/never before on record"
singular language of the sun-lit faces
mistress of the blinded sages
music keeps us up on who we are
poets who have come back
& who have gone the hard way
hard-schooled horn players/passionate strummers
& the forever jazz singers
like the glittering tambourines & razzle dazzle
all these disparate lovers of the stolen powers
the well kept secrets/the long sung celebration
of this is the music
knowing we can't be us
& live it less.

January 1979, Brooklyn, NY.

EXPANDABLE LANGUAGE

Vorbatim from an interview with Jonathan David Samuel "Papa" Jo Jones

Everybody knows that
the elder was watching
seen us coming from way far
you could hear his music
over six decades if you lived
that long but you didn't
not then he would say
you wanted him to say
but he wouldn't
he knew what you wanted

I watch the reflection
of the bridge he said
in the painting of the bridge
when the sun sets
his back turned
to the bridge even now

I haven't heard no music
since Kansas City
and I fear no one
cause I fear God
but I have heard 'em cook
and I am crazy thank God
for that
I am no one
I'm 50 people I once knew

He could see us from way far
he only spoke looking through
your hair past your brain

to your safe zone
where you can be trusted
had no need to talk to you
of time you did not live

I could indulge you
but you can hear me
playing behind Lady Day
I know nothing
'bout slavery
I was born free
and heard the blues
when they asked me
was the Count colored
all I could say was very

You see I played music
with folks who could stand up
with nothing but the rhythm

1985, New York Hospital.

34

IT'S TIME FOR THE RHYTHM REVUE

it's Saturday morning
and I wanna dance
it's time for the Rhythm Revue
I don't wanna riot
don't wanna riot
it's Saturday morning
and I wanna dance

I know there's only minutes left
have to tune in
find out if it's a riot in LA
or if we can still dance
to Teddy Pendergrass
& songs we hummed before
they made love stories
called "Damage"
Al Green is crying,
Aw baby, did you mean that?

was the jury hung in LA?
did they acquit somebody in LA?
will we burn it down on Saturday
or dance to the Rhythm Revue
the not too distant past
when we thought we'd live on?

"I'm the one who loves you," Curtis sang
and yet we came up in flames
you don't have to ask about a riot
lit timbers fell down all around us
chaos, yes, I told the kid

I was there for some of that
yes, I've seen a mob

"what's your name
I've seen you before
what's your name
may I walk you to your door?"
these were dumb lines
that is their charm

don't wanna riot in LA
don't wanna be shot down
"what's your name
is it Mary or Sue
what's your name
do I stand a chance with you?"
it's Saturday morning and I'm angry too
I learned my name is Rodney King
long ago and I'm waiting
waiting for a verdict
radio doing four-part

this boy asked me on Friday
had I ever seen any violence
which kind I asked? which kind?
the civil kind, he said
what's that? I said
the LA kind is what he meant
Sam Cooke is singing
"let the good times roll
we gonna stay here till we soothe our souls"
a helicopter roars over the house
a dozen police cars squat in front of my post office
this very morning

the air is bright and gorgeous
a kid from Brownsville asked me
had I ever seen any violence
that's why I clean my house
listening to songs from the past
times when no one asked anyone
if they'd seen a town burn
cause baby everybody had.

1992, Brooklyn, NY.

CICATRIX
For the Art Ensemble of Chicago

apparition of my early markings
the music walks through my day & ordinary day ways
resurrection of the flesh/of the carving of my skin
I have come to be the dancer within
come the route of Chicago/New Orleans
my carousel days of rhythm n blues
come the route of a creole gal in flamingo satin
who wears the azure & indigo feathers of her beginnings
through swamp she clutches the plumes of a bird
    of Guinée
a remembrance of initiation
they carved lines/painted dominoes & sunbursts
spoke words of designation/to be cast afar
knowledge of world/to raise/to move
sun bathes the skin of today's placid face
sets me free/raises gently chin to cloud
feel the stick of dots yellow, green, white
working beads about my eyes
through half-eyes I feel you
with parted lips I breathe & savor
the ritual streets of Reese/the clay of home
my initiation, my initiation
breathe & savor the palm wine/the leopard whispers
feathers & razor pins/hollow marimba sounds sunset
    on dust
dust under dancing/whirling disc of my golden cloth
whirling disc about my neck/my wealth & scars/my
    initia-
my initiation
sunset whirling dust & firecast mauves
sound the clash, the clang the cowrie's chuckle

the low tone of dusk/the blue entrance/love
walk/lip talk/moan/the snail curls at my ear
my intia- my initiation
remembrance rings/sings alone with eyes glaring
into mine/thru the patterns of colors/of markings
raised in language for the seer
like the freed bird walking/touching earth to prove
the gift of wings/I raise my head bound in beads
& walk flesh alone into this night
silence of my body creeps from hearing to the dusk.

1976, DC Space, Washington, DC.

HE DIDN'T GIVE UP/HE WAS TAKEN

he didn't give up/he was taken
he was possessed
he was only of the night
his back flew him up & down
up & down/he was gone
and only of the night
darkness & the powers of music had taken him
he did not know/a thing
god just kept leaping out of his fingers
& his back bent
threw him back & forth
his mouth was all a singin
the night had taken all but sound
up & down/he was thrown
out his belly/pushed out his back
he belonged to the night
with only a faint sensation of blessing
a heat enclosing his head
like giant hands pressing
even the rain took him
gleaming in the slant
sound still leapt
a shaft of rain he stormed
he flooded & leapt upon his demons
sound punished/sound confessed
sound made a balance
of the slipping/swishing rain
he bent & stood up against
the rain had taken everyone
there was only night black
black gleaming rain
& the gutter

& the ecstasy of his screaming
his teeth chewed the air
& spit it out night black
a man a man a man a man
a man a man a man a man

1975, unknown hornplayer outside the Village Vanguard, New York.

AS I FLY OVER THIS TIME

For Dianne McIntyre

as I fly over this time
rising over only this
so much painted suffering
unseen grimaces and stares
among spruce greens
these few forests left
all of us trying to be alone
quiet and blind

I see soldiers in bus stations
with colored names
polaroid shots
their girlfriends chew gum
smile wide

in all this silver of sky
like stars these wheels
car gears lampshades
electrical refuse
zen oiled and greased
the believers now so many
now so tired of the sad songs
the endless yearnings for war
and more and more

dumb cries I sigh
trying to get out of town
I am writing on the wall
it will be painted over
like all the songs
once outside
but as I fly over this time

Dianne is dancing
touching the far reaches
leaping and teaching
she strokes and struts the air
none of us stumbles
or fears our lives
steel beams and rail tracks
strike an E-flat, B-flat, A
E-flat, B-flat, A
Dianne is dancing
no one can handle the hostages
terror is abandoned
because of light
breaking in leaves
because the center is gone
we are still breathing
and the swing is our bodies

ca. 1978, 15th Street, New York.

43

the "Iron Man" sat with gone eyes/a witnessing body
& a bad case of sky high low cold cerebral blues
the lady in orange came lit up with love and night
    blueness
David came with a gold horn/a copper suit
& Joann's Green Satin Dress
Fred came to do bizness/Bobo came disguised as the
    Black Knights
Drum & Bugle Corps
& Hamiet Bluiett came from Lovejoy, Illinois 62059
the truth came down twice/I was caught in the middle
when it catches me I'm tasty & dangerous like one more
    for the road
it laid me out/it buried me after it worried me
it put ice to my temples & spewed out steam
it was rough/like playing with crackers in Cairo
like playing hard to get on Cottage Grove
it was rough like making love in wet grass
a heat that makes a chill of remembrance
when the bottom dropped & the floor sank to the metro
I fell in David's bell/where melody is personal
the drum skin began to sweat burlesque
I heard it plead: please the ghosts/cast the flowers
the poem asked what it is to be a man
it was a rough blues/the truth came down twice
& squeezed me like a lemon/skinned me
& left a tingle there to taste
after such music there is only the quiet shimmer
the glow of eyes being handed back their sight

April 27, 1977, The Rogue & Jar, Washington, DC. The players: David Murray, Hamiet Bluiett, Charles "Bobo" Shaw, Fred Hopkins. The poet: Ntozake Shange.

C.T.'S VARIATION

some springs the Mississippi rose up so high
it drowned the sound of singing and escape
that sound of jazz from back
boarded shanties by railroad tracks
visionary women letting pigeons loose
on unsettled skies
was drowned by the quiet ballad of natural disaster
some springs song was sweeter even so
sudden cracks split the sky/for only a second
lighting us in a kind of laughter
as we rolled around quilted histories
extended our arms and cries to the rain
that kept us soft together

some springs the Mississippi rose up so high
it drowned the sound of singing and escape
church sisters prayed and rinsed
the brown dinge tinting linens
thanked the trees for breeze
and the greenness sticking to the windows
the sound of jazz from back
boarded shanties by railroad tracks
visionary women letting pigeons loose
on unsettled skies
some springs song was sweeter even so

ca. 1978, 15th Street, New York.

45

the idea that they think must scare people to death
the only person I ever met from southeast DC
was a genius who stabbed her boyfriend
for sneaking up on her in the kitchen
she was tone deaf and had no ear for French

she once burned her partner in bid whist
for making a mistake
but she would wait on a corner at night
for a guy with a suit and briefcase
who didn't want to be seen with her in the day

he wanted to buy me a Bentley
because he didn't want to be black
I wanted her to get him in the kitchen
prove she wasn't so deaf
she couldn't hear the dirt flying
but she was smarter than me
and graduated early and left town

my friend the child prodigy
always looked to me like Billie Holiday
the genius from southeast DC
told me she was a junkie
with the wrong class of friends
so was Billie Holiday she would point out

and so were the kids at the rock lounge
they'd never heard of Anacostia
or cared why the singer was missing some teeth
made me think of kids from Queens
yelling at Garland Jeffreys for an encore

"nigger, get back out here"
I wondered why they played reggae
when their rock 'n' roll made the punks so crazy
wondered why they didn't just get them in the kitchen
while they had them
slam dancing each other to the floor

the punks jumped on the stage
and dove into their friends
let their chains beat their thighs
the crowd thought death
in two-minute intervals
heavy metal duos and creaming murder

the band of twelve-year-old rockers
wished they could do it
come like that on the refuse
of somebody else's youth

1982, CBGB, New York.

47

imagine now & know the old renegades
in this room/like ghosts
imagine Thebes & this stuff here/this music
dig gold miners leaving a strange land
going to their own land to dig gold
to send to another land
dig all the ghosts/outraged minstrels
painted in the folkore of their time
dig piano players who went to Paris
in the first war & came back
to play in Louisiana whore houses
dig an old guitar player who couldn't spell
and signed his life away with an X
to a cat in a bus station with $50
dig your ancestors/in this room
who have given up the cares of their moments
& look now smiling only upon your souls
you in this room

July 28, 1977, Storyville, New York. The players: Malachi Favors, Joseph Jarman, George Lewis, Roscoe Mitchell, Famoudou, Don Moye.

A MAN'S TAILOR/DAKAR

the sewing shop is very cool
the owner wears shades
and French trousers
African men with taste
for Patato, Totico & *guaguanco*
like the taxi driver
who could tell you
someone shot Chano Pozo
in a bar in Harlem in '48

the young men work the machines
like potters find the center
they work circles, snails
and recenter the cloth
leaves and diamonds
the mosaic floor of a mosque
concentric, hypnotic
like prayers or mantras
the stitches are very close
the lines quite straight
and quite curved

the owner starts to bargain
the client pretends he's shocked
they are having a sport
and both will do business
robes drift in a clothes line breeze
the needles buzz
while the pedals hum
salsa is rocking
and the machines are swaying

December 16, 1987, Dakar.

T-MONIOUS

We'll still be there
In our flattened-seventh hats
Rootie tootie shoulder slips
Saluting, tipping and caning
Where "it's always night"

Some folks will keep missing
The notes not there
But lots will hum anyway it comes
Brilliant corners jut and glide
Out of mouths and bopping bent knees
Slow dragging our minor styles, sly Miles
The broken hearts and time

For Ruby, Nellie, Pannonica
Four fingers down one up
Ninths pyramid of course
Hide under his slap-and-fly feet
And laugh too
While analysts go in circles
Forget the retributions
Dealing us like they dealt the rest

We'll still be there
Where it's always night
Doing more Monk
Not just bipbop not just jazz
Or whatever made him say
"Well, you needn't" that way
The secret's in Billie's photo
Or the back roads of divine healers
Gone the way of God

It's on the corner of 63rd
In the crackling applause
At the Apollo
For a kid who played "all wrong"
He always won hands down flat out

Not just history not just Trane
No not what we heard about
What we heard
Just what we hear
It always being night
We'll still be there
Dancing the dissonant logic
The loneness
Just playing music
He speaking to himself
Really paying us no rabbitass mind
Digging what himself was doing
T-monious and "al-reet"

February 17, 1982, 122nd Street, New York.

LEAVING GOREE

we were crushed on the pier
I lost touch
trampled by undertow
thieves pressed
a hand ran across my back
I shouted
fled to the side
the soldiers shoved us
onto the boat

I'm holding myself
with tight hands
down narrow steep steps
into the hull

one stretches his leg
to see if it is broken
his friend rubs it
and checks the bones
I rub the cuts
on my feet
my knee cap smashed
against iron
it will be black
by morning
all I can do
is crouch over
I cannot lift
my head
where a woman is talking

last time we saw her
I did the talking
for those who cannot
understand her tongue
this time all I can do
is look sideways
toward the infant
tied to her back

she has some beads as before
and she is smiling
not as arrogant
not as proud
the baby could be
the prophet
he is a jewel of heaven
tranquil and shining
his face just taking shape
his head just sitting straight

why does she not talk
the woman asks my friends
they do not understand
I do not respond
she gets my eye
"tired" is the only word I have
she looks hard at me
without suspicion for the first time
without curiosity
or a made-up mind

"I too am tired"
she gestures at her stomach
to make it look bigger

she points to the baby
on her back
and at her feet
"see for yourself"
her eyes say
I point at mine
she nods at me
while my friends wonder
what she wants

a tear starts at my eye
but I look at the ceiling
and then across the room
two Bambara women
have been watching, smiling
gold teeth gleaming
black lips and bare shoulders
they sit like mountains
these women
more beautiful than any I've seen

one opens her mouth
which is huge like a fortress
and so she sings
a song of her village
the other claps her hands
and soon we are nodding
and the boat is rocking

they just keep staring
and saying the words to me
and then to my friends
at first only "so beautiful"
is all I make of it

and they are staring
and singing right at me

an old man begins patting
a bit of wood like a guitar
a balafon player watches
his instrument is gone
but he is hearing the music
and lightening his face
letting go of something
he was carrying around

and so the song goes
and the women are standing
flirting and gesturing
clapping and smiling
they call the men dada
and tell them the story
of their village in Gambia
some ways away

"and now this is Senegal"
the leader is saying
"we are come to Senegal"
is all I can make out

curling their voices
like muezzins and ramhorns
they saved me
they made me
see their smiles

when they have sung
to the others

that they have sung us
this song
all the young girls join in
having known the song all along
I could not move
as the song went round
but I was so content
as the song went down
I later told one
how beautiful it was
was it truly?
was all she said.

December 1987, Dakar.

LAWN CHAIR ON THE SIDEWALK

there's a junkie sunning himself
under my front tree
that tree had to fight for life
on this Brooklyn street
disease got to its limbs
while still young

I had to brace the tree
so it could stand
wash it down with curatives
just as now I tamp the earth
around the hyacinth
dug up every night
by a hungry animal
who rips it from its bed
and leaves it half-trampled

he has a lawn chair and radio
playing old time jazz
sun warms his swollen hands
shade cools his scarred ruddy face
it looks as if he were in a fire
but only a florid disease
has burned his skin
fire that kills the blood

the man is sunning himself
with caution
taking in the spring heat
along with the small shade
of the still young tree

his chair faces the corner
and behind his shades
his eyes seemingly adrift
with the music
are watching for the dope man

ca. 1992, Brooklyn, NY.

ZOOM (THE COMMODORES)

I once drove to Atlantic City
in the middle of the night
I crept thru a thunderstorm
for the Spinners/Harold Melvin & the Bluenotes
& motherfathersisterbrother
otherwise known as MFSB
I lost my voice for love
ever since doo-wop I've been weak
for the sound of Philadelphia
it's well known
I remember the Howard/the Apollo
a few roadhouses
& even Ester's Orbit Room
sweaty funky overweight underbuilt joints
where you could buy to satisfy
any of your senses
where romance flourished in the garish pink lights
and sweet night of the Coasters/the Tempts
& sweet Smokey's Miracles
oh! where romance had a chance/was the chance
the only chance any of us had
young college students don't like to discuss it
young poets eschew it
but after the Club Harlem & sandy crab cakes
under conk lights & dawn drunks
across the street I found the Commodores
known for the profound rhymes of our times
like "it's slippery when it's wet"
the tasteless fleshiness of the seventies
can be redeemed if you just learn to zoom
zoom saves love & rescues romance
zoom "I'd like to take just a moment

& dream my dreams"
zoom you Commodores
with all the footlight ardor & corn
with all the foolish sincerity of a man
who don't care who knows/bout his jones
his love/his woman/his sweet thing
his squeeze/his weakness
his nose that a truck could run up
his crush/his sun/his moon/his starship
the sunshine of his life/the apple of his eye
his queen/his dream/his ZOOM
you can tell me all that/I don't mind
zoom I'm with you Commodores
talking trash is one of the lost arts
of making love & giving humanity a break
zoom I'm with you Commodores
cause you meant it/and you loved her
and you did fly to that good woman
who waited/who waited for her baby
her man/her jones/her sweet daddy
her good thing/her love/her only one
her sun/her moon/sweet nights in June
her honey/her sweetheart
her ship that was comin in/her zoom
you Commodores
maybe you are the best of us
that can love & believe
all our foolish triteness
& the way we can't talk when it's important
& the love that can keep death waiting
til we see those eyes one more time
zoom I love you Commodores
I wanna fly away from here too
zoom I love you

when you call in the night
cause you couldn't catch a cab
cause you see things in the dark
zoom I love you when you use subterfuge
to get me alone/when you drop hints/or drop by
when you promise me everything cause I'm so divine
zoom I love you
cause you won't say no/cause you don't want to go
cause it's so cruel without love
give me the tacky grandeur of Atlantic City
on the Fourth of July
the corny promises of Motown
give me the romance & the Zoom

1977, Washington, DC.

THULANI DAVIS (b. 1949) is an interdisciplinary artist and scholar whose work includes works of poetry, theater, journalism, history, and film. Her engagement with African American life, culture, and history is distinguished by poetic economy, passionate musicality, and an investigative concern for justice. While a student at Barnard College, the Virginia native was "schooled" for her first spoken word performance by Gylan Kain and Felipe Luciano of the Original Last Poets, jumpstarting a life of performance that would have her put words to music by Cecil Taylor, Joseph Jarman, Juju, Arthur Blythe, Miya Masaoka, David Murray, Henry Threadgill, Bernadette Speach, and others. Living in San Francisco in the '70s, she joined Third World Communications, collaborated with Ntozake Shange, and worked for the *San Francisco Sun-Reporter*, reporting on stories such as the Soledad Brothers trial and the Angela Davis case. Returning to New York, she continued to incite radical political thought as a reporter and critic for the *Village Voice* for over a decade. This journalism experience blazes through her historical fiction and her other writing, breathing anecdotal life into the experiences of actors of American history who have remained unknown as a result of bondage and decades of unjust erasures. Davis has collaborated with composer Anthony Davis, writing the libretti for the operas *X, The Life and Times of Malcolm X*, and *Amistad*, and wrote the scripts for the film *Paid in Full*, as well as several award-winning PBS documentaries. In 1993, she won a Grammy for liner notes for Aretha Franklin's *Queen of Soul: The Atlantic Recordings*. She is the author of *My Confederate Kinfolk* and the novels *1959* and *Maker of Saints*. Her earlier poetry books are *All the Renegade Ghosts Rise* and *Playing the Changes*. She is an ordained Buddhist priest, founded the Brooklyn Buddhist Association with her husband Joseph Jarman, and is currently an Assistant Professor in the Department of Afro-American Studies and a Nellie Y. McKay Fellow at the University of Wisconsin.

Poet, novelist, playwright, and performer JESSICA HAGEDORN was born and raised in the Philippines and came to the United States in her early teens. She is the editor of numerous anthologies and author of several books including *Dogeaters*, winner of the American Book Award and a finalist for the National Book Award. In the '70s and early '80s, she collaborated with Thulani Davis on multimedia performance pieces presented at downtown venues such as The Public Theater and The Kitchen.

Critic and essayist TOBI HASLETT has written about art, film, and literature for *n+1*, the *New Yorker*, *Artforum*, the *Village Voice*, and other publications.